AGAINST PARITY

A RESPONSE TO THE "PARITY"
VIEW OF THE CHURCH
ELDERSHIP

About the author
B S Poh was born in Malaysia in 1954. Brought up in a pagan background, he was saved by God's grace through faith in Jesus Christ while studying in the United Kingdom. He returned to Malaysia to become a lecturer in a university for six years, founded the first Reformed Baptist Church in the country in 1983, and was imprisoned for his faith from 1987 to 1988 for a period of 325 days. He is the pastor of Damansara Reformed Baptist Church (DRBC) in Kuala Lumpur, a contented husband, a thankful father of four sons, and a happy grandfather. He earned the PhD degree in Electronics Engineering from the University of Liverpool, UK, the Diploma in Religious Study from Cambridge University, UK, and the PhD degree in Theology from North-West University, SA.

AGAINST PARITY

A Response To The "Parity"
View Of The Church Eldership

B S POH

GC

Published by
Good News Enterprise

AGAINST PARITY: A Response To The "Parity"
View Of The Church Eldership

Copyright ©Boon-Sing Poh, 1999, 2006

ISBN: 978-983-9180-23-7

First published in Gospel Highway magazine:
1999
Second imprint: 2006
This edition: March 2017 (Re-formatted.)

Unless otherwise indicated, Scripture quotations
are from the New King James Version, copyright
1979, 1980, 1982 by Thomas Nelson, Inc.

Published by:

GOOD NEWS ENTERPRISE, 52 Jalan SS 21/2,
Damansara Utama, 47400 Petaling Jaya,
Malaysia.
www.rbcm.net; www.ghmag.net

Printed by:
CreateSpace, an Amazon company, United
States of America. Typeset by the author using
TeXworks, the memoir class.

.

To

all Reformed Baptist brethren

who love "the gates of Zion".

Contents

Contents

Contents

PREFACE

The substance of this book was first published in the magazine *Gospel Highway*, in 1999, as a response to the book, "In Defense Of Parity", by S. Waldron, *et. al.* The latter was itself a response to my book, "The Keys Of The Kingdom: A Study On The Biblical Form Of Church Government". The present book may be understood without prior reading of the other two books.

The book "In Defense Of Parity" is still actively circulated, and is also published on the internet. This reprint of "Against Parity" retains the substance of the original except for minimal changes. References to "The Keys of the Kingdom" now include, in square brackets, pages of the re-formatted edition of February 2017 (distributed on www.amazon.com). It is shown that "In Defense Of Parity" fails to make a convincing case for itself.

The present writer takes no pleasure in controversy. This book is intended to help, not to provoke. If the Reader is led to a more settled view of the church eldership, by returning "to the law and to the testimony", this modest book would have accomplished good. May the Triune God receive all the glory! Amen.

B S Poh,
Kuala Lumpur, March 2017.

One

GENERAL CONSIDERATIONS

A book entitled, "In Defense Of Parity", subtitled, "A Presentation of the Parity Or Equality of Elders in the New Testament", was published by "Truth For Eternity Ministries" in America, in 1997. It consisted of a collection of essays on the subject of the parity of the church eldership, written by four contributors – Samuel E. Waldron, Gregory G. Nichols, James A. Hufstetler and David J. Chanski. The first three are pastors of the Reformed Baptist Church of Grand Rapids, Michigan, while David Chanski is the pastor of the Providence Reformed Baptist Church of Minneapolis, Minnesota, a daughter church of the former. [Most of these men have moved.]

1. GENERAL CONSIDERATIONS

The book sets for itself two goals: (i) as polemic, "to address recent attacks on and defend the doctrine of the parity of the eldership" (p. 7); and (ii) positively, to present what the authors believe to be "a balanced, biblical view of this subject" (p. 8). The contents of the book, set forth in 138 pages, are as follows:

Chapter 1: "Parity and Diversity in the Eldership: Parity", by G. Nichols.

Chapter 2: "Parity and Diversity in the Eldership: Diversity", by G. Nichols.

Chapter 3: "A Contemporary Reaction to the Parity of the Eldership", by S. Waldron.

Chapter 4: "An Exegetical Defense of the Parity of the Eldership in the New Testament", by S. Waldron.

Chapter 5: "A Careful Exposition of 1 Timothy 5:17", by S. Waldron.

Chapter 6: "An Historical Examination of the Parity of the Eldership in Independency and John Owen", by D. Chanski.

Chapter 7: "The Baptist Confession of 1689 and the Parity of the Eldership", S. Waldron.

Chapter 8: "The Call to the Ministry and the Parity of the Eldership", by J. Hufstetler.

Chapter 9: "The Practice of the Parity of the Eldership", by D. Chanski.

Any reader of the book will quickly realise that it is primarily a response to the book "The Keys of the Kingdom", written by the present writer. The name of Poh Boon Sing is mentioned critically in every chapter, including in the Preface, except for the two chapters by Greg Nichols. A copy of the book was sent "hot from the press" to me by D. Chanski. This followed an earlier letter to me from Chanski, co-signed with Waldron, in which was stated, "I am writing primarily to lodge a protest and offer some criticism concerning some of the things you wrote, and also to make you aware that some Reformed Baptist pastors here in the States intend to publish a response to 'The Keys of the Kingdom'."

I have attempted to remain level-headed while reading the book, with the intention of amending my view on the eldership, and even of completely replacing it, if necessary. After reading through the book three times, I have not been convinced by the view it propounds. (By the time this article is completed, I would have read through the book at least another time.) My initial reaction had been to leave the issue alone and let the readers form their own judgement on it. However, the manner of its espousal is such that I am convinced of the necessity of replying to it. The circumstances in my life have not permitted me to write a response earlier.

1.1 General observations

1.1.1 The spirit

The spirit of the book is hardly eirenic, although the authors evidently attempt to restrain themselves. I hazard the guess that the spirit of the book is the result of the following: (i) The authors have taken my criticism of their view personally; (ii) The authors have engaged in selective and cursory reading of my book; and (iii) The differences in age, experience and personality among the contributors. Indications of these will become apparent as we proceed.

In my book, I have said in the Foreword, "The reader will have to pardon the author if, at places, the preacher in him shows!" I am primarily a preacher, by calling and vocation, and only secondarily a writer. The language of speech is usually different from that of writing, but I have always attempted to write the way I would speak. Furthermore, preachers often use hyperbole to gain the attention of the hearers and to drive home a point, although I would hasten to add that the point being made must be factual. It is the *manner* of presentation that has been commonly dubbed "the preacher's hyperbole". Although I was generally aware of the possibility of being picked upon in this area, and hence the qualifying statement in the Foreword of my book, it came as a disappointment and a surprise that this really happened. One of the contributors to the book on "parity" took exception to my stating that the 1689 Confession is "crystal clear" in making a distinction between the pastors and ruling elders (pp. 4, 116, and three times on p. 125). Clearly, that writer is not only challenging the clarity of the issue, but is also unhappy with the expression "crystal clear".

The same writer takes exception to my remark that those who hold to the "parity" view "have had an influence that is out of proportion to their small numbers". In a footnote, he said, "It is at least my impression that most of the largest Reformed Baptist Churches in America and a host of smaller churches hold our view. In fact, we believe that the vast majority of those churches which hold formally to the 1689 Confession in America espouse our view. We further think that any fair survey of the rest of the world would probably contradict his assertion that we are in the minority (p. 120)." The tentativeness of the contributor's claim that those who hold to his view are not in the minority is obvious. In fact, in reference to my book, which propounds a different view, he said, "His book appears to represent the views of a number of Reformed Baptists and is being given some 'press' by them not only in America, but in the British Isles (p. 51)." In reference to my view that there is a distinction between the teaching elders and the ruling elders, the same writer admits: "He is not alone in holding or assuming this distinction. This distinction is held or at least assumed by many in their views of church government (p. 63)." The book further identifies my view of the call to the ministry as "the traditional view", which these advocates of "parity" attempt to counter (pp. 4, 131).

I stand by my remark that those who hold to the "parity" view are in the minority, since it is based on my perception of the situation in United Kingdom, America and other parts of the world. Let those who so desire make a survey of the matter, but I will not be tempted to "number Israel" (2 Sam. 24:10; 1 Chron. 21:1, 7-8). Afterall, we do equally hold to the conviction that at the end of the day, it is the authority of Scripture that must hold sway. What is saddening is that the contributors to that book take my criticism of their view so personally.

In another place in the book, it is stated, "At best, Poh gives a poor caricature of the views of such Reformed Baptists as Sam Waldron and A. N. Martin based, we presume, on ignorance of their actual teaching and practice (p. 100-

101).” It needs to be noted that my references to Sam Waldron and A. N. Martin were rather minimal, and restrained, in a quarto-sized (“standard sized”) book of over 400 pages with print-size “point 11” (smaller than the normal “point 12” print). While not pretending to be a scholar, I was writing a book which could be used “as a manual for church-officers and a textbook in seminaries” (Preface). As such, I had to quote sources to support my points, which included Sam Waldron and A. N. Martin, who happened to be among the few who have actually published on the “parity view” (in print and on tapes). I know of others who have propagated that view in Malaysia, Singapore, Australia and Philippines, but they have not published their view in print (as far as my knowledge goes).

The book characterises my book (or, more accurately, some sentences in my book) as “reactionary” (p. 56). An extract from my book reads as follows: “As will be shown below, the current fad to restore a plurality of elders, coupled with the emphasis on the equality of all elders, in Reformed Baptist circles, is in reality a struggle over the validity of the office of ruling elders.”

The writer claims to be mystified by the “derogatory language” of the phrase, “the current fad to restore a plurality of elders”. How that phrase constitutes derogatory language is mystifying to me! If anything, that contributor and his colleagues appear to be aware that their book is reactionary in character! (Along the same line, Chanski and Waldron expressed their indignation, in their letter to me, that I have asserted that those who call all elders pastors are "extreme". What I actually said in my book – and please remember that it is being isolated from its context – is, "Other churches, some of them very influential, believe in the 'equality of elders' and carry this to an extreme, calling every elder 'pastor', p. 5 [4]." Carrying a belief to an extreme is different from saying that those who do so are extreme. Why should it be construed as the latter?)

Then, offence is taken over the fact that I associate the "parity" view with "heavy shepherding", being "cocksure", and "the Diotrephes spirit" (p. 58). I have argued soberly on the dangers that are inherent in the "parity" view, and then proceeded to discuss the damage it may cause to other churches. This is based on actual situations in this country and elsewhere which I know of. The contributors, however, have chosen to take it personally and retaliated by using the language of ridicule and scorn. If only they had kept their cool, and read everything carefully and in its total perspective, the outcome would have been happier! For example, I mentioned the danger of the "Diotrephes spirit" in connection with one who is agitating for the "parity" view to be accepted in his own church (p. 155 of my book). This is different from saying that those who are already in a "parity" setting are Diotrephes, or that they are promoting the "Diotrephes spirit". The perceived charge of being "Diotrephes" has clearly stirred up the ire of these men, for it is raised again in other parts of the book (pp. 135, 138, and also in the letter to me).

Consider further the following statements, - which aim at criticising Poh Boon Sing and his view of the eldership:

"The following pages also reveal that a sense of personal irritation is skewing Poh's thoughts (p. 58)."

"All this might sound as if the other elders are allowed little or no initiative... Poh will have to pardon us for thinking that he is very ambivalent about other elders taking initiative in *the pastor's* church!" (Emphasis original, pp. 60-61.)

"Poh Boon Sing's interpretation of John Owen's church polity is inaccurate, especially on the key matter of parity in the eldership. His portrayal of the views of other Reformed Baptists is also flawed. Regrettably, he has evidently studied neither well (p. 114)."

One cannot help it but ask, "Is such language really necessary?" The last quote also shows that the writer has either missed, ignored or taken advantage of the statement in the Preface of my book: "Research has been hampered by the ab-

sence of a good theological library in this part
of the world. God has mercifully provided the
basic books needed,..." It may be that Poh Boon
Sing has not read as much as that contributor,
nor studied as well as him. Suffice to say here
that Poh Boon Sing has read all the relevant articles and books listed in the bibliography, which
number over 100 items, and he is always ready
to learn and read more. (For the record, I studied through John Owen's "The True Nature Of A
Gospel Church" no less than 15 times.)

So much for the spirit of the book. We now
make some general observations on its methodology or approach.

1.1.2   The approach

In any debate, the contending parties are constantly switching roles as the proponent and the
opponent. The proponent will put forward his
case by two basic steps: first, that of stating his
view; and, second, that of supporting his view.
These two steps may be called "proposition" and
"proof". In its simplest form, the "proof" consists of the presentation of the relevant proof-
texts, which should speak for themselves. Or,
more commonly, it will involve the presentation
of the "premises" and "the scheme of inference"
(or pattern of reasoning, which leads to the conclusion), based on the Bible texts, and the cor-

rect rules of biblical interpretation. The conclusion is, of course, the "proposition" which is being proved. The proponent will also need to restate his opponent's view and then refute it. The "restatement" serves the purpose of showing that he has understood the position of his rival, and sometimes of casting it in its true light so that the refutation will be easier and clearer. The four steps of a debate may be portrayed schematically as follows:

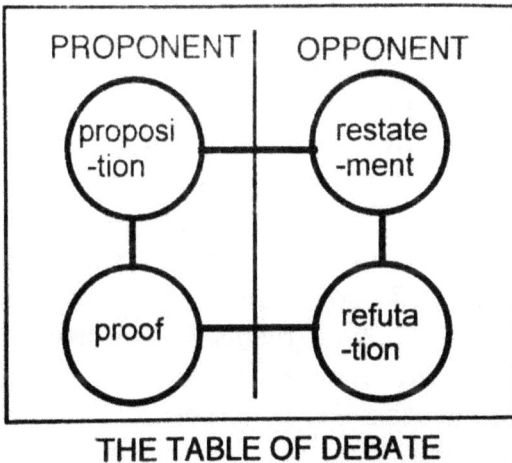

THE TABLE OF DEBATE

It can be seen that the "table of debate" has four legs. If any of the legs were missing, the table would not be stable. If only two legs are left, it will topple easily. If only one leg is left, the case has collapsed! An example of the two-legged position is found in my book (p. 260 [265]), in which there are the "proposition" and the "refutation", but there is no "proof" offered, while the "restatement" is rendered void by a *misrepresentation* of the opponent's view. Needless to say, in advocating my view in this article, I shall be presenting all four "legs", with emphasis on two of them, namely the "restatement" and the "refutation" of my opponents' view. At this point, we only wish to present some observations on the approach adopted by Sam Waldron and his colleagues, *vis-a-vis* "the table of debate".

Throughout the book, the contributors have ignored my proofs. They refuse to counter the biblical considerations that I have put forward in proof of my position. In short, they do not engage in "refutation" and, instead, throw forth an abundance of verbal barrage and insinuation – perhaps with the intention of outshouting their opponent, and also of putting off the readers from reading my book for themselves. When dealing with the spirit adopted by the book above, we have given examples of the sort of language that is employed. Here, we give a few more examples of how verbal barrage and insinuation take the place of the "refutation" process:

"It is difficult to restrain a sense of injustice at the many misrepresentations of the plurality and parity of the eldership as we hold it to be found in this paragraph (p. 57)."

"It is also difficult to restrain a sense of indignation at the cavalier disregard for the biblical mandate for humility and a servant spirit among the elders (p. 57)."

"But unfortunate as these paragraphs are, the following two or three paragraphs are worse (p. 57)."

"Poh manifests his confusion further on page 169 [170] (p. 59)."

"There is similar inconsistency and ambivalence with regard to the elders and pastor in Poh's description of how elders' meetings should be handled (p. 60)."

'Do New Testament pastors really stand in the tradition of the prophets in terms of their divine call? Are they really "personally" commissioned by Jesus Christ to be His ambassadors? Does this mean they receive direct revelation as the prophets did concerning their calls? Does this mean that a light appears from heaven and a voice calls out as it did to Saul of Tarsus? I am certain Dr. Poh would not want to say such things (p. 130).'

These substitutes for a proper "refutation" may appear cogent to the unwary reader simply because the contributors have misrepresented and distorted my view, by outright assertions and selective quotations. In other words, the contributors have not only failed to present the "refutation", but also the "restatement" in the debate. The verbal barrage is aimed at the straw-men they have erected.

For example, in the last quote above, the writer is countering a *conclusion* of mine that the pastor needs the divine call of God to be in the ministry; that he needs to be personally commissioned by Jesus Christ to be His ambassador; that there is this inner compulsion in him to proclaim the word. The *conclusion* is in effect the "proposition" of my case. A proper refutation would be to show that my *premises* have been wrong, or that my *scheme of inference* has been defective. I have argued in my book (p. 115 [113]) that the context of Ephesians 11:4 shows that the "pastors and teachers" are preachers of the word who are mentioned in the same breath with apostles, prophets and evangelists. I have further amplified my arguments in another chapter of the book (pp. 192-197 [193-199]), which the contributor seems not to have read, showing that the pastor is an ordinary officer of the church who must fulfil the qualifications of eldership in the New Testament, at the same time that he is a minister of the word and stands on the same platform with the apostles, prophets and evangelists. It is these arguments that should have been refuted. Instead, that contributor has chosen to scornfully insinuate that my view necessarily involves the pastors receiving extraordinary communication from God.

Another example should suffice. One contributor of the book quoted a passage from my book:

"The ministry of the word should have *primacy* (that is, the supreme place, the pre-eminence) in the life of the church. It should have *priority* (that is, being earlier, occupying the position of greater importance) over other important matters. Of the two types of elders, the teaching elders have the priority over the ruling elders."

Based on this quote, it is asserted that I believe, "that elders who labour in the word have a higher degree of authority than elders who do not labour in the word (p. 108)." The assertion is pressed home with the further statements: 'Owen never argues that, on the basis of the "superiority" of the *teaching function*, the one who labours in word and doctrine has greater *governing authority*. Poh evidently senses this when he attempts to enlist support for his assertion from Owen (p. 109).' These are not the only places in which the assertion is made that I believe that pastors have the greater *governing authority* compared to other elders (pp. 99, 100, 112, 134). This assertion, however, is a blatant misrepresentation of my position.

In the passage quoted (above), I was arguing for *the priority of the ministry* which, of course, cannot be dissociated from *the minister*. I was not dealing with "governing authority", which I see as distinct from, although closely related to, "teaching authority". With John Owen, I hold to the view that Scripture makes a clear distinction between the authority to teach and the authority to rule – the two "keys of the kingdom of heaven". With Owen, I hold to the view that all the elders, both the teaching and ruling ones, are equal in the sense that they occupy the same office of ruling. I further asserted that all the elders rule in unity, as a body. The teaching elders are the ones who *execute* the authority of teaching, while the whole eldership has the *responsibility* over both the teaching and the ruling of the church. This is expounded in some detail under a chapter in my book entitled, "The Unity of the Eldership" – which chapter seems to have been by-passed by that contributor.

A major point in my book is that, historically, three views of the eldership have been practised in Presbyterianism, which are today being duplicated in Reformed Baptist circles. I have called these views the "Presbyterian View", the "Independent View", and the "Absolute Equality View". In the "Independent View", to which I subscribe, the minister of the word is an elder who shares the same office of rule with the "ruling elders", while in the "Presbyterian View", the minister of the word holds an office distinct from, and above, that of the ruling elders. Sam Waldron and his colleagues have, throughout their book, failed to state my view clearly, apart from making a passing reference to it (p. 63). Instead, they have lumped the Presbyterian and the Independent views together as the "three-office" view (pp. 32, 63, 90, 91). In fact, the distinct impression is given that I actually hold to the three-office view of church government, in which the church officers consist of the minister, elders, and deacons. Sam Waldron and his colleagues chafe over the fact that I have labelled their two-office view (consisting of elders and deacons, with no distinct position of the minister of the word) as the "Absolute Equality View". The propriety of using this name has been shown in my book (chapter 5), and will be discussed again below. Here, we wish only to show that they have obscured a major point in my view of the eldership – namely, that there are basically two offices in the church (those of elders and deacons), in which are two categories of elders (the teaching elders and the ruling elders).

We summarise this section on "General Observations", which covers *the spirit* and *the methodology* of the book on "parity". The authors of the book on "parity" have been unable to conceal their ire at my book, "The Keys of the Kingdom". They have retaliated by pouring scorn and ridicule on my view of the eldership. As far as the methodology goes, they have failed to present a proper "restatement" and a proper "refutation" in the debate. Instead of the "restatement", my position has been misrepresented by ignoring the relevant points, making untrue assertions, and presenting selective quotes. Instead of the "refutation", they have engage in throwing verbal barrage at, and making insinuations about, my view. Two "legs" are missing from their "table of debate". In effect, what they are left with is only one of their two declared objectives: to positively present their view of the eldership.

It remains now for us to make a more detailed analysis of the book. We shall focus on the methodology and the substance of each contributor. We consider first the doctrinal chapters, and then the historical ones.

1.2 Analysis of contents

1.2.1 Chap. 1. "Parity in the Eldership", by Greg Nicols

To his credit, Greg Nicols is the only contributor who does not engage in diatribe in his two articles. He positively expounds his view of the eldership by highlighting two characteristics – "parity" and "diversity".

In his first article, he establishes the concept of "parity" from Scripture, showing that the parity in the eldership is a parity of office. He argues from the various relevant passages that one who is a bishop (or overseer) is a presbyter (or elder), and also a shepherd (or pastor). In my book, I have argued out the case that all pastors are elders but not all elders are pastors. One of the arguments I used in support of this is that the verbal form "to pastor" is used in Acts 20:28 and 1 Peter 5:2, in reference to the work of elders in general, while the noun "pastors" is used in Ephesians 4:11, in reference to the ministers of the word. Nicols ignores this argument, leaving it to Sam Waldron to deal with in a later part of the book.

Nicols next shows that parity in the eldership entails equality in *authorisation* and *representation*. The elders are equally authorised by and accountable to Christ. As a body, they are authorised to govern the entire life of the church according to the word of God. The elders also represent Christ before the church, and represent their church before the other churches and before the world.

The practical implications of parity follow: (1) Parity implies that all the elders should participate in visiting and counseling the flock. (2) Parity implies that all the elders should participate in interviews of prospective members. (3) Parity implies that all the elders should be included in setting church policy. (4) Parity implies that each elder should get pastoral oversight from the eldership as a body. (5) Parity implies that the elders are equally eligible to lead the observance of the sacraments. (6) Parity implies that the elders are equally eligible to represent their church in associations. (7) Parity implies that each elder must grasp sound doctrine and be apt to teach and defend it.

To be noted in the list of implications is the absence of any mention on preaching. One would have expected Nicols to say, "Parity implies that all the elders *should participate in* (or *should be included in*, or *are equally eligible to*) preaching regularly from the pulpit." Statement No. 7 is a rather lame replacement for what we would expect to be the more natural implication of parity. It is in fact not an *implication*, but a *requirement* of Scripture. The *implication* should be rather that all the elders are eligible to preach regularly from the pulpit.

Sensing the likelihood of this being picked up by the careful reader, Nicols attempts to cover up by quoting Dabney, who defended exactly this point (p. 23). Dabney said:

"Perhaps the most plausible objection... against our theory is this, that if you teach the ruling elders are among the scriptural presbyters, then you can no longer draw any consistent line between them and ministers, you must make them all preachers..."

Dabney's defense, however, is not strictly applicable to Nicols's case, because Dabney was a Presbyterian who held to what I have called the

"Independent View" of the eldership, in which there is a clear distinction between the teaching elder and the ruling elder. In his defence, Dabney went on to assert that the function of the ruling elder is just as truly and as purely a teaching function as that of the preacher, that he rules by teaching, that his whole authority is exercised through the inculcative process. This, of course, answers well the question why the ruling elder, who is among the scriptural presbyters, should be "apt to teach" when he *does not preach regularly in the pulpit*. To Dabney, the ruling elder "is never to mount the pulpit" simply because he is a ruling elder and not a minister of the word. In Nicols's view of the eldership, there is no sharp distinction drawn between the teaching elder and the ruling elder. Dabneys defence can be harnessed to support the point that all elders are required to have the qualification of being "apt to teach", but it does not answer the question why all the elders should not have equal eligibility to preach.

1.2.2 Chap. 2. "Diversity in the Eldership", by Greg Nicols

In his second article, Nicols demonstrates the principle of "diversity" by the same steps as before. He first shows from Scripture that there is such a concept as "diversity" in the eldership, based on 1 Timothy 5:17, Romans 12:6-8; 1 Corinthians 12:28, 31, and 1 Peter 4:10-11. All elders have the same office, rank, and authority. They all belong to the same ruling body of church officers. Yet Scripture teaches that the eldership displays a diversity of vocation (or career), of proficiency, and of giftedness.

These three areas of diversity are next discussed. Much space is devoted to the discussion of "diversity in vocation", revolving around the vocation of the minister. The caution is given that we are dealing with the ordinary vocation of the pastor-teachers, and not the extraordinary ones of apostles, prophets and evangelists. In virtue of their ruling office, they may be called bishops, pastors, and elders. In virtue of their life's work and vocation, they are preachers, teachers, and ministers of Christ, of the word, and of the gospel. It is not unbiblical to address them either in terms of their office, or their vocation, or a combination of both. Little space is given to the discussion of the call to the ministerial vocation. It appears that Nicols is leaving it to Hufstetler to deal with the subject more thoroughly in a later chapter. The essential duties and aims of the ministerial vocation are then laid out.

Of interest to us is the fact that Nicols's discussion on the "diversity in vocation" revolves exclusively around the vocation of the ministry of the word. He has said, "Whereas some elders spend their day labouring at farming, engineering, carpentry, medicine, or law, other elders labour full-time in the study, exposition, and proclamation of the Scriptures (p. 27)." Why aren't the other vocations discussed? It seems clear that Nicols is here responding – consciously or unconsciously – to the emphasis of Scripture on the preaching vocation. True, the other elders labour at other vocations, but theirs are *mundane* vocations – vocations shared by other man who are not elders, and even by those who are not Christians. Preaching is a *special* vocation, different from the ordinary vocations. Its uniqueness should not be lost sight of. It may not be classed together with the mundane vocations. Nicols and his colleagues have chosen an inappropriate term – "the diversity in vocation" – to describe the eldership, for it does not do justice to the high position given in Scripture to the one vocation of the ministry of the word.

Nicols goes on to discuss "diversity of proficiency and honour in the eldership", based on 1 Timothy 5:17 – "Let the elders that rule well be counted worthy of double honour, especially those who labour in the word and in teaching." He argues that the adverb "kalos", translated "well", is comparative. "Though all men qualified to be elders rule with a modicum of competence, some elders rule with marked proficiency (p. 36)."

This understanding is open to question, but we will reserve it for later when we consider Sam Waldron's exposition of 1 Timothy 5:17. Nicols next talks about "special respect and appreciation" which must be shown to the elders who rule well. He says, "All elders are very valuable to the church, and she should highly esteem them (1 Thess. 5:12), but elders doing a good job are doubly valuable, that is, emphatically more valuable, and she should increase dramatically her esteem for them. This primarily applies to her vocational pastors, her preachers (p. 38)." Here again, the preachers are singled out as those deserving an abundance of honour, different from the elders who hold other vocations. As mentioned already, the term "diversity" does not bring out this truth. Nicols goes on to show that the "double honour" shown to preachers who rule proficiently should include adequate financial remuneration – which point we have no problem with.

Nicols ends the second section of his article by discussing "diversity of giftedness in the eldership". This is followed by the final section, in which he enumerates some of the practical implications of diversity, which include: (1) Diversity implies that some elders may have a larger share of the pulpit or lectern. (2) Diversity implies that some elders may take a larger share of visiting and counseling. (3) Diversity implies that some elders may have a higher profile in church administration. (4) Diversity implies that some elders may have a wider influence or recognition. (5) Diversity implies that all pastor-preachers need not have the same "job description". (6) Diversity implies that some are gifted to teach and preach who have not the office of elder. (7) Diversity implies that all pastor-preachers need not necessarily receive the same salary.

To be noted is the fact that the principle of "diversity" is now worked out to its logical conclusion – namely, that the special place accorded to the ministerial vocation in Scripture is diluted to become just one of a number of vocations, just one of a number of gifts. Therein lies a major point of difference between my view and that of Nicols and his colleagues. In my view, due cognisance is given to the special position of the preacher, at the same time that the twofold division of the office of elders are noted. And there is no neglect of the fact that there is a parity of office. I have described my view with the principles of "rule by elders", "the priority of the ministry", and "the validity of ruling elders". Together with the other principles which I have established in my book, a completely self-consistent description of the biblical eldership emerges: "rule by elders", "the priority of the ministry", "the validity of ruling elders", "the unity of the eldership", and "rule with consent". The diversity of gifts, the diversity of tasks, and the consequent diversity in influence, respect and salary are all subsumed under these principles. These are mere practicalities that each church has to wrestle with in its own situation. These are not essential to a true description of the biblical eldership.

We repeat. In the view of Nicols and his colleagues, no special place is accorded to the ministry of the word as required by Scripture and no recognition is given to the twofold division of the tasks of the elders – namely those of ruling and preaching. We are not saying that they are not aware of these scriptural points. In the discussion of their view, Nicols has concentrated on the vocation of the ministry of the word, as we have pointed out above. He has also noted the two divisions in functions of the elders, saying, "Scripture delineates various pastoral gifts. Some gifts relate mainly to the ruling office, some primarily to the preaching vocation. In Rom. 12:6-8, the ability to teach (12:7) and to exhort (12:8) relate mainly, though not exclusively, to the preaching vocation. The ability to manage or govern (12:8), relates chiefly, though not only, to the ruling office. In 1 Cor. 12:28-31 Paul first lists three ministerial vocations which God placed in the church, apostles, prophets, and teachers. Apostles and prophets were restricted to the founding of the church (Eph. 2:20). Teachers are permanent, set by God in the church in every generation. I take it that Paul refers mainly to official teachers, elders who labour in the word, whom he denominates in terms of their vocation. Yet I concede that the phrase may encompass, not only preachers, but, in Hodge's words, all 'uninspired men who had received the gift of teaching' (pp. 42-43)." Nicols and his colleagues are insistent in maintaining that teaching is a gift that is tied to a vocation, but not to office. We would have more to say on this later, when we come to Hufstetler and his view of "the call". That aside, the fact is that they are aware of the two categories of duty – ruling and teaching – even if they insist that it is no more than a matter of gifts or vocation (pp. 42-43, 71, 86, 106). Their description of the church eldership, by the principles of "parity" and "diversity", however, does not indicate this biblical distinction.

1.2.3 Deficiencies of "parity" and "diversity"

Perhaps this is the right place to point out that their adoption of the two principles of "parity" and "diversity" is a departure from the usual approach of advocates of their view, who would use the "parity-plurality" combination, instead. The contributors to this book have themselves used the "parity-plurality" combination elsewhere. In this book, however, they emphasise the characteristic of "diversity" instead of "plurality", although they occasionally lapse into using the term "plurality" (pp. 22, 97, 117, 135). By emphasising "diversity", they avoid having to answer for the weaknesses inherent in the "parity-plurality" combination which, I believe, has played no small part in creating havoc in weaker churches that have tried to implement it. I have pointed out these weaknesses in my book (pp. 152-159 [152-161]), and it has not gone down well with our esteemed friends. It is hardly fair for them to shift the emphasis to a "parity-diversity" combination in their book and yet pour forth such wrath upon me for pointing out the weaknesses of the "parity-plurality" system!

Is the "parity-diversity" system substantially different from the "parity-plurality" system? The difference is not in substance, but in emphasis. It is my contention that the difference in emphasis is enough to offset to some extent the weaknesses of the "parity-plurality" combination, but it is still not good enough to constitute the biblical model of the church eldership. We have seen that it fails to give due weight to the special place of the ministry of the word, and it fails to indicate the ruling-preaching distinction in the eldership. This is because the terms "parity" and "diversity/plurality" are too general and too vague. They describe the *consequential* characteristics, not the *essential* characteristics, of the eldership. "Parity" is the consequence of there being only one office of rule. "Diversity" and "plurality" are the consequences of there being some elders who rule by "labouring in the word and doctrine" and others who rule without "labouring in the word and doctrine". Describing the eldership by the principles of "parity" and "diversity/plurality" is like describing a cup of coffee as "a drink that is black and sweet". While this is a true description of coffee, it is not good enough. There are other drinks which are both black and sweet. One can think of "coke", and many other drinks, which fit that description. Furthermore, one will have to qualify himself by saying, "I want black coffee, not coffee with milk or cream added," or, "I want percolated coffee, not instant coffee," or, "I want coffee with sugar, not plain black coffee."

It is a fact that there are marked differences among those who subscribe to the "parity" view. The Brethren would preach in rotation, and not have a "minister", nor a "leading elder". Some Reformed Baptists would have the elders take turns to be the leading elder, while others would appoint a permanent leading elder on the basis of seniority, gift, or some other criteria. Some others would believe in the traditional "call" to the ministry, while others would rely only on the qualifications listed in the 1 Timothy 3 and Titus 1 to choose a minister. Some churches would have preaching elders only, while others would have ruling ones as well. All these would describe their views by the terms, "parity" and "diversity/plurality". These terms may, in fact, be used to describe my view of the eldership! I believe that the minister is an elder who shares the same office of rule with the ruling elders, and they rule as a body. There is parity! I also believe that ruling elders should be appointed to help the minister in governing the church. There is plurality! Yet my view of the eldership is substantially different from that of Nicols and his colleagues!

Consequential characteristics are *descriptive* in nature and should never be made prescriptive. When they are made *prescriptive*, disaster is in the offing! Consider the likely outcome of making the principles of "parity" and "diversity/plurality" prescriptive. When a church is told, "Make sure that there is parity among the elders!", everyone's attention will be focused on the rank, authority and eligibility of each elder relative to the others. When a church is told, "Make sure that there is diversity among the elders!", everyone's attention will be focused on the gifts, tasks, and influence of the elders. When a church is told, "Make sure that there is plurality among the elders!", everyone's attention will be focused upon the need to appoint more than one elders, all for the sake of "plurality". We see then the potential disaster to a church that makes these principles prescriptive. Much as we would like to avoid it, the attention is focused upon the individuals and the power they have, or do not have.

The outcome is not the same when the principles in my model of the eldership are made prescriptive to a church. Furthermore, my model cuts the roots off the hierarchy that is encountered in Episcopacy and some Presbyterian denominations, and also steers clear of the single-pastor-plural-deacons situation seen in many independent churches. This is not to claim that churches which practise the Independent model of the eldership will be free from problems, for anything right, true and good in itself can be abused, misunderstood, or misapplied. What we are claiming is that the "Independent View" of the eldership takes into account all the relevant biblical data in a way not done by other views.

Two

DOCTRINAL CONSIDERATIONS

We are making a critique of the book "In Defence Of Parity: A Presentation Of The Parity Or Equality Of Elders In The New Testament". We have commented on the book in general, and have given a detailed analysis of the first two chapters, by Greg Nicols, one of the contributors of the book. It is with a heavy heart that we continue analysing the remaining chapters. But continue we must, lest we are mocked for not being able to finish what we have begun.

2.1 Chap. 3: "A Contemporary Reaction to the Parity of the Eldership", by Sam Waldron

Chapter 3, which purports to present my view of the eldership, turns out to be an exercise in mud-slinging and nit-picking. Poh follows Owen to a fault. Poh contradicts himself. Poh makes astounding claims. Poh is full of inconsistency and ambivalence. Poh uses derogatory language. Poh is unfair to historical facts. Poh misrepresents other people's views. In short, Poh is a very, very bad boy! Waldron seems bent on presenting me and my view in a bad light. After reading the chapter, the reader will still be no clearer as to my view of the eldership. Is my view that difficult to understand? Is my presentation of it in the book, "The Keys of the Kingdom" so difficult to grasp? If so many people have found no difficulty reading my book, why should Waldron find it so confusing? I suggest that the answer lies in Waldron himself!

It is distressing to find so many points that need answering. We will single out only a couple of them as examples. Waldron claims that I have read the 1689 Confession of Faith through the lens of the Savoy Platform and John Owen, citing pages 121-126 [120-126] of my book (p. 55). A quick check will show that, in those pages, I was arguing from the First London Confession of 1644 and the related Separatist Confession of 1596, and not from the Savoy Platform. Furthermore, he throws a low kick, saying, in parenthesis, "and by the way ignoring differences between the 1689 and the Savoy Platform". But I have taken into consideration the differences between the 1689 Confession and the Savoy Platform in the relevant parts of my book (pp. 100, 128, 317 [100, 129, 324]).

Waldron also claims that I have the tendency to define office in terms of function when, in fact, that is my quarrel with the advocates of "parity" (p. 114 [112] of my book) – namely that they tend to define office in terms of function! In his presentation of the "parity" view, Greg Nicols has himself listed the practical implications of "parity" and "diversity" in terms of functions – visiting and counseling the flock, interviewing prospective members, setting church policy, etc. (pp. 19-22, 45- 48). Stating it mildly, Waldron appears to have forgotten my extended treatment of the concept of "office" (pp. 90-93 [88-92]), and its practical implications (pp. 169-174 [170-176]).

Waldron ends the chapter by identifying a number of points of disagreement between his view and my view, which he claims will be addressed in the subsequent chapters. These points all revolve around whether there is a distinction between the teaching elders and ruling elders.

2.2 Chap. 4: "An Exegetical Defense of the Parity of the Eldership in the New Testament", By S. Waldron

In this chapter, Waldron makes a study of the words "shepherd" and "teacher" by considering various passages in turn. We first make some observations about his methodology.

2.2.1 Waldron's methodology

Firstly, Waldron employs the method of repeated assertion to strengthen his case. The assertion is constantly made that there is no distinction between pastor-teachers and the other elders. The converse of the statement is also constantly asserted, namely that all elders or bishops are pastors. This is done from the very outset of the chapter when he shows in a diagram the English translation of the terms "poimen", "episkopos" and "presbuteros", followed by the "official distinction" of these terms. Under the "official distinction", the assertion is made, in capital letters, "ALL SIX OF THESE ENGLISH TERMS DESIGNATE ONE AND THE SAME OFFICE IN THE

NEW TESTAMENT". This is followed by the equations: "The Pastors=The Bishops=The Presbyters", and, "The Shepherds=The Overseers=The Elders". But assertions do not constitute proof, and the mere repetition of the assertions will not add material value to the assertions themselves.

Secondly, Waldron considers the relevant passages in isolation from one another, drawing conclusions from them without regard to the whole. In the exegesis of any Bible passage, one would normally engage in analysis by dissecting the passage according to its natural divisions and then studying the constituent parts in detail. This is a legitimate, useful, and necessary procedure. However, whatever conclusions that are drawn from each of the parts must take into account the context of the whole passage. This every careful Bible expositor knows. A parallel may be drawn here. In studying all the relevant passages on the eldership in the New Testament, we must draw conclusions that are consistent with the totality of the New Testament teaching on this matter. This, I believe, Waldron has failed to do.

Thirdly, Waldron engages in a species of "arguing from the silence of Scripture", which is fraught with danger. One can think of the argument that since there is no explicit statement in the Bible that God is one, and yet there are three persons who are completely God, it follows that the doctrine of the Trinity is not true! An example will be seen in his treatment of Ephesians 4:11 below.

2.2.2 The contents

We move on to the contents of the chapter. There are two main sections. The first deals with the word "poimen" (pastor) and its relatives, and the second with the word "didaskalos" (teacher) and its relatives. The passages considered in the first section include Ephesians 4:11; Acts 20:28, 1 Corinthians 9:7; and 1 Peter 5:2. The passages considered under the second section include, among others, James 3:1; Romans 12:7; 1 Timothy 3:2; and 1 Timothy 5:17. It will not be necessary for us to comment on all of Waldron's treatment of the passages, for each of them ends with the refrain, "No distinction is made between the office of teaching elder and the office of ruling elder." Instead, we will consider his treatment of Ephesians 4:11, which he recognises as the only passage in the New Testament in which the noun, "poimen", occurs in relation to an ecclesiastical office.

Waldron admits that the "pastor-teachers" in Ephesians 4:11 are the only permanent office (not just a vocation) in the church (p. 65). He goes on to make the amazing assertion, "There is clearly no explicit contrast instituted here between pastor-teachers and 'ruling elders' in this passage. This passage provides no evidence by itself for a distinction between pastor-teachers and other elders in the church. It cannot, therefore, be a proof-text for that position which posits such a distinction." Waldron would want us to conclude from Ephesians 4:11 that the "pastor-teachers" are a reference to all the elders of the church. But the stark fact is that the passage makes no mention of elders. By his own arguments, we could say there is clearly no explicit mention that these pastor-teachers are elders, and therefore they cannot be elders of the church at all! We will not resort to such argumentation, however, and contend only on legitimate principles.

The fact that the "pastor-teachers" are mentioned together with the apostles, prophets and evangelists in the same verse show that it is a vocation *and* an office. The subsequent verses confirm that it is the office and vocation of *preaching* that is in mind here. Elders who are not full-time in the ministry of the word are excluded from this catalogue of officers. Who exactly are this category of church officers called "pastor-teachers"? Do they occupy an office different from that of elders? If they do, there will be three permanent offices in the church – those of pastor-teachers, elders, and deacons – since the other two offices are mentioned elsewhere in the New Testament. This conclusion, however, will not tie up with the facts that: (i) the qualifications of only two offices are listed in 1 Timothy 3; and, (ii) only two categories of officers are mentioned as officers in the church, in passages such as Philippians 1:1. If there are only two permanent offices in the church – namely those of elders and deacons – who are the "pastor-teachers" of Ephesians 4:11 (and, we would include, the "teachers" of passages such as Acts 13:1; 1 Corinthians 12:28; and James 3:1)? Are they one and the same as the elders? If they are one and the same as the elders, then, either: (i) all the elders are full-time preachers, or, (ii) some elders are full-time preachers while others are not. We know, however, that there may be elders who are not full-time preachers but who nevertheless are rulers in the church (Acts 20:34-35; 1 Tim. 5:17). We conclude, therefore, that some elders are full-time preachers while others are not. The pastor-teachers of Ephesians 4:11 must be elders who are full-time preachers.

Since the noun "pastor" is used only here, and that in reference to the office and vocation of teaching, it is surely legitimate for us to conclude that the teaching elders are the "pastors and teachers" of the church. We are not oblivious to the fact that the verb "to pastor" is used in reference to the basic duty of all elders in Acts 20:28 and 1 Peter 5:2. We have no problem with that at all because the church is described as the flock of Christ, who is the Chief Shepherd (1 Pet.

5:4). The Lord Himself had described His followers as sheep (e.g. John 10:27), and referred to them collectively as a flock (Lk. 12:32; Jn. 10:16). The task of taking care of His flock is therefore that of "shepherding" when seen in relation to the object (the flock), and that of "overseeing" when seen in relation to the subject (the elders). The chief way by which the flock is shepherded is through the ministry of the word ("My sheep hear My voice...", Jn. 10:27), and that is the task of the under-shepherds, the pastors of the church (Jer. 3:15). The responsibility of the elders, therefore, encompasses the two basic areas of ruling and teaching – the two "keys of the kingdom of heaven" (cf. Mt. 16:19; 1 Pet. 2:25). All the elders execute the rule of the church, led by the pastor (or one of them, if there are more than one pastors), and the pastor(s) execute the task of teaching, under the responsibility of the whole eldership. And remember that we are not excluding the ruling elders, and for that matter, other gifted brethren in the church, from preaching as and when the occasions require, according to their ability.

We see, then, that reserving the title of "Pastor" for the teaching elder is not a mere matter of terminology, as Waldron and his colleagues make it out to be (pp. 29-32, 74). I have, in the early part of my book, said, "Other churches, some of them influential, believe in the 'equality of elders' and carry this to an extreme, calling every elder 'pastor'." If it were a mere matter of terminology or form of address, I would not have been too bothered. It is what lies behind the practice of calling all elders "pastors" that is worrying. The name used bespeaks the system of eldership practised. This I have made clear in the paragraph in which that sentence occurs, and in the subsequent unfolding of my book.

2.3 Chap. 5: "A Careful Exposition of 1 Timothy 5:17", by S. Waldron

This is the longest chapter in the book – longer than the two chapters by Nicols combined. Waldron begins the chapter well by stating that, in regard to 1 Timothy 5:17, "We must allow it to speak for itself in its native context. We must not manipulate it early in the interpretive process so as to make sure that it raises no questions about deeply held convictions (p. 76)." He opens up the text under two headings: (i) Its Historical and Grammatical Interpretation; and, (ii) Its Practical and Ecclesiastical Implications.

2.3.1 Financial support

As one proceeds in the study of the chapter, it becomes clear that three main points stand out. The text itself reads, "Let the elders who rule well be counted worthy of double honour, especially those who labour in the word and doctrine." The first point Waldron establishes is that "double honour" means "ample material or financial support", "given as a mark of the value and esteem of the church" (pp. 79, 80). The text, and the verses following it, come immediately after the earlier section, namely verses 3-16, in which the apostle discusses the "honour" that must be shown to true widows. In that earlier section, the apostle refers to the financial support of the widows. In the later section, the apostle refers to the financial support of the elders. The church appeared to have been unduly concerned about the support of widows, while exhibiting a tendency to neglect the support of the work of the gospel.

The situation of the church implied in 1 Timothy 5 could have developed from the original state of affairs indicated in Acts 20:17-38, in which the elders seemed to have worked in their secular vocations and were not financially supported by the church. Based on the Acts 20 passage, Waldron repeats the assertion that there was a plurality of elders in the one church in Ephesus, and that the elders were also called overseers and shepherds (p. 82). (We have made the point that the Acts 20 passage does not call the elders "shepherds", but describes their work as that of shepherding.) The conclusion made is that the text of 1 Timothy 5:17 is not contrasting between honouring all the rest of the elders and double honouring well-ruling elders. Rather, the contrast is between honouring widows and double-honouring well-ruling elders. The well-ruling elders are to be counted worthy of being given ample material or financial support.

2.3.2 Well-ruling elders

I have no problem with Waldron's first point. My problem is with his second point, which is that there is an implicit contrast in the phrase "well-ruling elders". The contrast is not between elders who rule well and elders who rule badly, for that would imply that all who are not worthy of double honour would be viewed as ruling badly. Rather, the contrast is between elders who rule well and elders who are generally good and qualified. Waldron refers to the definition of the word "well" given in one lexicon (Bauer, Arndt and Gingrich): (1) beautifully, finely, excellently, well; (1a) rightly, so that there shall be no room for blame, well, truly; (1b) excellently, nobly, commendably; (1c) honourably, in honour, (1c) in a good place, comfortable; (1d) to speak well of one, to do good; (1e) to be well (of those recovering health). From this, he says, "Clearly, this definition shows that the word is susceptible of conveying a superlative force. The well-ruling elder is, then, the excellently ruling elder (p. 85)." He further claims that the usages of this word in the New Testament "appears to have this force", citing a number of passages. He concludes by saying, "It is better, then, to recognise in the adverb, well, a superlative or comparative sense which is intended to contrast not good and bad, but good, better, and best (p. 86)."

One cannot help wondering whether the word "well" carries a superlative or comparative sense. Waldron first says that it carries a superlative force. He then expands it to "a superlative or comparative sense". He has made it so elastic that it now contrasts good, better, and best! We would challenge the very first premise that the word is meant to be a contrast, regardless of whether it is a contrast between good and bad, or between good, better, and best. The more natural sense is that it is descriptive. It is an adverb ("kalous") which describes the verb "to rule" ("proestemi"). Together, the two words function as an adjectival phrase, qualifying "elders". All the elders are meant. They all are well-ruling men. If there is any contrast at all, it is between the well-ruling elders and the widows mentioned in the earlier section of the passage (1 Tim. 5:3-16). Widows are worthy of honour. Well-ruling elders are worthy of double-honour.

All the Bible passages cited by Waldron in which the word "well" occurs actually shows that it is used descriptively and not comparatively (pp. 85-86). It describes the action performed. It does not compare the action, much less the person performing the action, with another. We reproduce here a random selection of his list, with the word marked in bold.

Matthew 15:7 – You hypocrites, **rightly** did Isaiah prophesy of you, saying,...

Mark 7:9 – He was also saying to them, "You **nicely** set aside the commandment of God in order to keep your tradition."

Luke 20:39 – And some of the scribes answered and said, "Teacher, You have spoken **well**."

1 Timothy 3:13 – For those who have served **well** as deacons obtain for themselves a high standing and great confidence in the faith that is in Christ Jesus.

James 2:3 – and you pay special attention to the one who is wearing the fine clothes, and say,

"You sit here **in a good place**," and you say to the poor man, "You stand over there, or sit down by my footstool." (The word "fine" is wrongly marked in bold when it should be the phrase "in a good place", which in the original was just "well". Instead of "in a good place", a better translation would have been "comfortably".)

2.3.3 Elders who labour in the word and doctrine

Waldron assigns very little space to making the third point, namely that there is a contrast between the well-ruling elders who engage in the public ministry of the word and those who do not. The nature of this contrast, which we believe is important, is not discussed. He is therefore able to combine this point with the second one, saying, "Paul's reference to well-ruling elders is not only implicitly contrasted with a larger circle of qualified elders, but it is also explicitly contrasted with a smaller circle within the circle of well-ruling elders (p. 87)." Financial support is to be focused in the inner circle, radiating outward as the necessity and ability of the church makes this appropriate.

In a brief exposition of 1 Timothy 5:17-18 in his earlier work ("A Modern Exposition of the 1689 Baptist Confession of Faith", p. 324-325),

2. DOCTRINAL CONSIDERATIONS

Waldron had mentioned only the first and third point, with no mention of the second. There were only two concentric circles – the outer circle which encompasses all elders who rule well, and the inner circle of elders who (are gifted to) work hard at preaching and teaching. In the present book, there are three concentric circles – the outer circle of qualified elders, the inner circle of well-ruling elders, and the innermost circle of elders who work hard at preaching and teaching. There is a contrast between the outer circle and the inner circle, and there is another contrast between the inner circle and the innermost circle.

We believe that it is incorrect to place the first contrast, if there is a contrast at all, together with the second contrast because the two are essentially different. The first contrast concerns the *manner* of rule – some elders rule well, while others rule exceptionally well. Put it to their differences in gifts, education, circumstances of life, and experience if you like (as Waldron does, pp. 86-87), and the contrast is still in the manner, or quality, of their rule. The second contrast, on the other hand, concerns the functions, or *type* of rule – some well-ruling elders work hard in preaching, while the others work hard in ruling only. Those well-ruling elders who have the additional task of preaching publicly are to have the priority in financial support compared to those who work hard only in ruling. Since the two sets of contrast are essentially different, how can they be placed together as though it is a mere matter of "good, better, and best"? A comparison is valid only in the same basic realm, involving the same basic characteristic. For example, we cannot say, "the orange is big, the pear is bigger, and the apple is sweetest!" Although the subjects of comparison are all fruits, the characteristics – namely, size and sweetness – do not match. In 1 Timothy 5:17, the subjects of comparison are the elders, but the characteristics – namely, how well they rule and what tasks they perform – do not match.

We have, for the sake of argument, assumed that there is an implicit contrast in the expression "well-ruling elders", as claimed by Waldron, and that has ended in difficulty. As argued out above, I do not see any *implicit* contrast between the elders in that expression "well-ruling elders". However, that is a relatively small matter compared to the contrast *explicitly* established by the word "especially". Waldron himself calls this an "explicit contrast". Any lexicon will show that "malista" ("especially") is the superlative of the adverb "mala", and carries the meaning "most of all, above all, especially, particularly, (very) greatly".[1] As used in 1 Timothy 5:17, it is clearly *comparative*, and not merely descriptive. It makes a comparison between two categories of elders.

49

2. DOCTRINAL CONSIDERATIONS

The comparison, moreover, shows forth the *priority* of one category of elders over the other. Furthermore, it is clearly *distinctive* – showing that the elders who "labour in the word and doctrine" are to be distinguished from those who do not "labour in the word and doctrine".

Waldron comes close to acknowledging these facts, but does not come far enough. He denies that the text teaches the so-called three-office view (p. 91). This, however, is irrelevant to the debate between us, for I hold to the same view as him in this. We equally reject the view that there is an office of minister or pastor which is higher in rank or authority than that of elder. Waldron, and his colleagues, however, have a habit of confounding issues with mere terminology. In denying the three-office view, Waldron objects to any special title being given to the privilege or function of the vocational pastor. We have already dealt with this point when discussing Ephesians 4:11 in Waldron's earlier chapter (chap. 4). The next point to be considered is, Does the text imply a distinction between ruling and teaching elders? Here, Waldron wavers. Again, he reduces the issue to a mere matter of terminology, raising irrelevant points along the way, and concludes that "the ruling/teaching elder distinction does

---

[1]Bauer, W., Arndt, W. F., and Gingrich, F. W., "A Greek-English Lexicon of the New Testament".

not adequately account for the diversity of Paul's conception (p. 92)". He would, however, admit to a distinction between the vocational pastor and the non-vocational pastor (p. 93). Of course, to Waldron, the term "pastor" means "elder".

It is clear that, in this lengthy exposition of 1 Timothy 5:17, Waldron is attempting to make out a case for the idea of "diversity in the eldership". His attempt consists of three steps: (i) diverting as much attention as possible to the matter of financial support when, in fact, this is not the problem between us; (ii) stretching the meaning of "well-ruling elders" to cover the idea that there is great diversity of gifts and functions among the elders; and, (iii) toning down the force and implications of the word "especially". That there is a diversity within the eldership no one will deny. It is such a general and obvious truth, which applies not only in the eldership but also in the church (1 Cor. 12). But is that all that may be gleaned from 1 Timothy 5:17, after such an expanded treatment?

2.4 Chap. 8: "The Call to the Ministry and the Parity of Elders", by Jim Hufstetler

In this short chapter, Hufstetler raises two main points: (i) the propriety of using the term "Absolute Equality View" in reference to his "parity" view of the eldership, and (ii) differences on the doctrine of the call to the ministry of the word. Hufstetler defines what he means, and does not mean, by the word "parity" (pp. 128-129). We hear him loudly and clearly. I believe I have correctly understood his position. Much of what he says I can agree with. However, there are differences between our views on these two main points, which we must address.

2.4.1 Propriety of the name "Absolute Equality"

First, the propriety of the term "Absolute Equality View" as a description of the "parity" view. In my book, "The Keys of the Kingdom" (pp. 139-152 [137-152]), I showed that the controversies over the eldership in Presbyterianism have crystalised into three distinct views: the Presbyterian View, the Independent View, and the Absolute Equality View. These views are also seen among Reformed Baptists today. Hufstetler claims that

I have not been really fair to historical facts by adopting such a classification, since various great Presbyterians had held to what I called the Independent View (p. 56). The essential characteristics of Presbyterianism, however, are: (i) a gradation of church courts consisting of committees of individuals; and, (ii) the local church being ruled by elders. Differences on the eldership does not constitute the essence of Presbyterianism. The question of fairness does not, therefore, arise.

In the Independent View, there is an equality of office among the elders. All the elders share the same office of rule, and they rule as a body. This view does not preclude a distinction between the minister of the word and the ruling elders. The minister is an elder who shares the rule, in equality, with the other elders. He has the added responsibility of preaching the word of God regularly. This added responsibility does not arise from the mere fact that he happens to be more gifted in public ministry. Rather, he is specially called by God to fulfil that responsibility. There are differences of opinion on the doctrine of the call, but all who hold to the Independent View of eldership sees the responsibility of the office of elders as extending over two distinct departments – that of ruling and that of teaching. These have been known, traditionally, as "the keys of the kingdom of heaven". The minister wields the two keys of teaching and ruling, while the other elders wield only the key of ruling. Put another way, the minister executes the duties of teaching and ruling, while the ruling elders execute only the duty of ruling. Having the *responsibility* of office is to be distinguished from the *execution* of the duties connected with that office.

In the Presbyterian View of the eldership, the ruling elders are not presbyters of the New Testament sense. Only the minister is such an elder. The other elders are only representatives of the congregation in the board of elders (i.e. the eldership). The minister is, therefore, of higher rank than the ruling elders. This is a three-office view, in which the minister, the elders, and the deacons constitute the church officers.

In the Absolute Equality View, there are two offices in the church – that of elders and that of deacons – just as in the Independent View. There is equality of office among the elders, just as in the Independent View. However, no clear distinction is made between the minister and the ruling elders. All the elders are equally eligible to all the duties that pertain to their office. The differences in gifts, training, opportunities, or desire for service, may result in one of them (or more) to be appointed full-time in preaching. The ministry is therefore a mere matter of vocation, arising from providential circumstances.

Since the Independent View holds to the equality of office among the elders, although making a distinction between the minister and the ruling elders, together with a distinction between the functions of teaching and ruling, an appropriate description has to be given to the other view of eldership which also holds to the equality of office among the elders. Both hold to "parity in eldership", but each sees it in a different way. The Absolute Equality View obviously carries "parity" to a higher degree, and hence the appropriateness of the word "absolute".

Then, we consider the view of John Owen on the eldership. In his discussion on the pastors of the church, which to Owen meant the teaching elders, he said: "...I will not deny but that in each particular church there may be many pastors with an equality of power, if the edification of the church do require it. ...And the *absolute equality* of many pastors in one and the same church is liable unto many inconveniences if not diligently watched against" (emphasis added; - Works, Vol. 16, p. 105). Owen was advocating that one of the many pastors in the church should have the "precedence for the observation of order" *ibid.*, p. 105), and warned against the danger of "absolute equality".

Commenting on 1Timothy 5:17, John Owen said this: "There are, therefore, two sorts of duties confessedly here mentioned and commanded;

– the first is ruling well; the other is labouring in the word and doctrine. Suppose that both these, ruling and teaching, are committed to one sort of persons only, *having one and the same office absolutely*, then are some commended who do not discharge their duty, at least not comparatively unto others; which is a vain imagination. That both of them are committed unto one sort of elders, and one of them unto another, each discharging its duty with respect unto its work, and so both worthy of honour, is the mind of the apostle" (emphasis added; Works, Vol. 16, p. 122).

Of interest here is not only Owen's defence of the distinction between the teaching elder and the ruling elder, but also his use of the phrase "having one and the same office absolutely". Owen held to the view that there are two offices in the church – that of elders and that of deacons – and there are two sorts of elders – one sort having the authority to teach and rule, while the other sort having the authority to rule only (*ibid.*, p. 42). Owen also believed that the first sort are further distinguished into pastors and teachers – but that is another story. To Owen, failure to distinguish between the two sorts of elders is tantamount to having one and the same office *absolutely*.

Finally, we note again that there are differences of opinion and practice among those who hold to the principles of "parity/equality" and "plurality/diversity". Hufstetler and his colleagues might want to emphasise diversity, sensing now the dangers and weaknesses inherent in "plurality". They might be able to avoid those dangers and weaknesses in their own churches, but there is no guarantee that the dangers and weaknesses will not surface in the future generations of believers. A comparison with Antinomianism is in order. There are theoretical Antinomians who object to the term "Antinomianism" being applied to them, for they would never condone lawlessness. In theological discussions, however, we use the term "Antinomianism" to describe those who deny the continuing relevance of the moral law in the Christian life – with no negative connotation implied or intended. I use the term "Absolute Equality View" advisedly, with no negative connotation implied or intended.

2.4.2 On the doctrine of "the call"

We proceed to the next main point raised by Hufstetler, namely, differences on the doctrine of the call. Hufstetler objects to the suggestion that those who hold to "parity" have difficulty reconciling their view with the doctrine of the call to the ministry. He first criticises my view, before putting forward his. The criticism, however, is directed at the *conclusion* that I have made from Scripture, rather than at the arguments that I have offered in proof of my position. Furthermore, my treatment of the doctrine was necessarily brief, in each place that it occurred, being secondary to the subject at hand. Nevertheless, sufficient material was presented to show that the ministry of the word has the priority in the divine economy. Following the older writers, I cautiously went as far as Scripture would permit by saying that it is not wrong to speak of the "office" of teaching elders and the "office" of ruling elders (pp. 117 & 145 [115-116 & 144] of my book) – a point criticised by Waldron (p. 63). We have seen already that Ephesians 4:11 lists pastor-teachers together with apostles, prophets and evangelists – men who were not only vocational preachers, but also church officers. Dipping randomly into John Owen, we find him saying, "These works of teaching and ruling may be distinct in several officers, namely teachers and rulers; but to divide them in the same *office* of pastors,..." (Works, Vol 16, p. 48, italics added); and, "Unto the call of any person unto this *office* of pastor in the church" (*ibid.*, p. 49, italics added). Owen looked upon the pastor as occupying an "office", although he has made it clear at the outset that, strictly speaking, there is only one office of elders, encompassing two categories of elders.

Hufstetler ends the chapter by declaring his view of the call, which is in fact different from the traditional view. Says Hufstetler, "The call to preach, or 'the call to the ministry', is not a call to a different office but is a vital and even primary function which is filled by every elder. Every elder is called to the ministry in the best sense of that word. All are called to serve Christ and His church. Some men may exercise a public ministry of the word while others exercise a less prominent ministry. This difference does not make the one with more public gifts to preach more of a pastor than elders who do not regularly preach the word publicly (p. 132)." Hufstetler ignores altogether the fact that there are strong advocates of the "parity" (i.e. the Absolute Equality) view who hold to the traditional view of the call to the ministry. (Need we name them?) He is able to avoid any contradiction with the idea of "parity" only by redefining the doctrine of the call! He is actually carrying the idea of "parity-and-diversity" to its logical conclusion – namely, to reduce the glory and uniqueness of the ministry of the word, accorded to it by Scripture, to just a vocation like other mundane vocations.

The difference between the Absolute Equality View and the Independent View cannot be clearer!

Three

HISTORICAL CONSIDERATIONS

We have completed the analysis of the doctrinal chapters of the book, "In Defence Of Parity: A Presentation of the Parity or Equality of Elders in the New Testament". We now proceed to the analysis of the historical chapters, before concluding this series of articles.

3.1 Chap. 6. "An Historical Examination of the Parity of the Eldership in Independency and John Owen", by Dave Chanski

If there is a master at misrepresentation, he is David Chanski.

He begins the chapter with "eirenic" words. He then attacks my suggestion that it is preferable to advocate "the validity of the office of ruling elders" instead of "plurality", claiming that it is a *de facto* retreat from the biblical emphasis. He supports his position of "plurality" by quoting John Owen, but does not make clear the fact that Owen was advocating a plurality arising from there being teaching elders and ruling elders – which is the position that I hold to! Put in other words, Owen's "plurality" is equivalent to my "validity of ruling elders", and different from Chanski's "plurality".

3.1.1 Parity

Chanski asserts that I believed in an hierachy of authority among elders, and that I incorrectly maintained that Owen granted a greater authority to the pastor than the ruling elder when it comes to the government of the church (p. 100). Where did Chanski get this blatantly untrue idea about my view? He bases it on my statement, "The pastors have the priority over the ruling elders," without reading carefully what I meant by "priority".

I have stated clearly in my book: 'The word "priority" includes the idea of "primacy" and more. The element of comparison is introduced when we speak of "the priority of the ministry".' The ministry of the word of God should have the primacy (i.e. supreme place, preeminence) in the life of the church. It should also have the priority (i.e. being earlier, occupying a position of greater importance) over other important matters. We are here comparing the relative importance of the officers in the church. ...Of the two types of elders, the teaching elder has the priority over the ruling elders (pp. 119-120 [118-119]).

I have also stated clearly, under the chapter entitled, "The Unity of the Eldership": '...the whole eldership is responsible for both the teaching and the rule of the church. The two "keys of the kingdom of heaven", the authority to teach and to rule, are committed to the eldership as a body. The teaching elders are the ones who *execute* the authority of teaching, but the whole eldership has the *responsibility* over that department of the government of the church (p. 174 [176]).'

3. HISTORICAL CONSIDERATIONS

To occupy a position of greater importance need not be read as "possessing greater governing power". As far as *governing* is concerned, all the elders (including both the teaching and ruling ones) share the same power, since they occupy the same basic office of presbyter.

Chanski then quoted from my book: "Some Reformed Baptists are advocating a view of the eldership in which all the elders are regarded as equal, with no distinction between them apart, perhaps, for the different functions they perform. To them, all elders are pastors."

To this, Chanski commented as follows: 'This is a fair representation of the doctrine of parity held by a number of Reformed Baptists. However, Poh does not regard this difference from his own view as either minor or innocent. He writes, "Some... [churches] believe in the 'equality of elders' and carry this to an extreme, calling every elder 'pastor'." He also caricatures their view of parity by calling it the "Absolute Equality View", and asserting that those who hold to parity believe "that all the elders are equal in authority *in every way*". One might be led to think that those who hold to parity teach that elders in every church must wear the same shoe size and part their hair in the same way. At best, Poh gives a poor caricature of the views of such Reformed Baptists as Sam Waldron and A. N. Martin based, we presume, on ignorance of their actual teaching and practice (emphasis added by Chanski, p. 100).'

Many things can be said about the paragraph above, but it will be a tedious exercise to attempt to do so. We will only point out his dubious way of presenting my view in this instance. In the quote of the phrase, "that all the elders are equal in authority in every way", he chooses to emphasise the phrase "in every way", without due attention given to "equal in authority". On the same page of my book from which this quote was extracted (p. 165), I immediately proceeded to elaborate by saying:

"This is based on the argument that in Acts 20:17, 28 and Titus 1:5, 7, the words 'elders' and 'overseers (or bishops)' are used interchangeably to refer to the same persons. From this, it is claimed that all the elders are pastors, and that the difference between the elders is only in the functions they perform. The different functions are distributed by mutual agreement among the elders. As far as authority is concerned, all the elders have equal rights to perform all those functions."

This is virtually a repetition of the earlier quote to which Chanski favourably commented as being "a fair representation of the doctrine of parity". It is clear that my emphasis was on "equal in authority". I have not been wrong in saying that the "parity" view believes "that all elders are equal in authority in every way", for they have equal rights to perform all the functions. This contrasts with my view in which all the elders are equal only in the sense that they occupy the same office of ruling, and share the same responsibilty (or "office-power", according to Owen, Works, Vol. 16, p. 37) over both the teaching and the rule of the church. The authority (or "rights", according to Owen) to teach and to rule are committed to the eldership as a body. Only the teaching elders *execute* the authority of teaching, although the whole eldership has the *responsibility* over that department of the government of the church.

3.1.2   No homogeneity

Chanski next attempts to show that, historically, there was no homogeneity in "Independent" church polity, particularly on the matter of plurality and parity in the eldership. John Owen insisted on the scriptural norm of the plurality of elders in each church and the scriptural validity of the office of ruling elders. In contrast, Benjamin Keach – a leading Particular Baptist of the seventeenth century – denied the continuance of the office of ruling elders. Chanski then garnered the support of the Baptist Association of Charlestown, South Carolina, which wrote in their "Summary of Church-Discipline" in 1774:

"The ordinary officers of the church, and the only ones now existing, are ministers and deacons (Phil. 1:1)... Ministers of the gospel, who are frequently called elders, bishops, pastors, and teachers, are appointed by Christ..."

We do not deny the fact that there was no homogeneity in "Independent" church polity. Equally, we should not deny that there was a clearly discernable "majority view" (if not a clear consensus) which constituted "Independent" church polity. By the process of selective quotation, Chanski is attempting to establish the former and subtly deny the latter. Much as we respect Benjamin Keach, we must not think that his view was representative of that of the early Particular Baptists. Another well-respected leader of the seventeenth century Particular Baptists, more senior to Benjamin Keach, who signed both the 1644 and the 1689 Baptist Confessions, was Hansard Knollys. His name appeared first in the list of church representatives who issued the 1689 Confession. In the area of eschatology, he was a convinced Fifth Monarchist, much to the embarassment of the other Particular Baptists. (The Fifth Monarchists believed that Christ would soon return to earth to inaugurate the millennial reign of the saints, the "Fifth Monarchy", and that it was legitimate to use force to establish the rule of Christ on earth.) We do not draw the conclusion from this that the 1689 Confession reflected a Fifth Monarchy view of eschatology, nor that it does not reflect the majority view of the Particular Baptists on eschatology.

To be noted is the fact that Independency, as espoused by John Owen, was sufficiently well established in the seventeenth century to the point that his book, "A Brief Instruction In The Worship Of God And Discipline of the Churches Of The New Testament", published in 1667, became known as "The Independents' Catechism". Owen's subsequent book, "The True Nature Of The Gospel Church", published posthumously in 1689, became the definitive exposition of Independency. Isaac Watts (1674-1748) made the observation: "The Baptists differ not from Calvinists in their doctrine, unless in the article of infant baptism. ...In church government they are Independents. ...the generalities of Independents follow rather Dr. Owen's notions: ...That the power of church government resides in the pastors and elders of every particular church."

Benjamin Keach's view of the eldership, published in 1697, i.e. two decades after the 1677 Baptist Confession (reaffirmed in 1689), must be seen as a departure from the majority view of the Particular Baptists. John Gill (1697-1771), who was a leading Particular Baptist in his days, and a contemporary of Isaac Watts, held to the same view of eldership as Benjamin Keach. That view, in which the office of ruling elders is denied, was to lead to the prevalent situation in later days, in which one pastor ruled with the help of many deacons.

The 1677/89 Confession was adopted by the Calvinistic Baptists of North America in 1744, and called by them the Philadelphia Confession of Faith. These Baptists believed in the scriptural validity of the office of ruling elders, even if they maintained that it was "wholly a distinct office" from that of the minister, as noted by Chanski (p. 105). The Charlestown Baptist Association, referred to by Chanski, may have been the oldest association in the South which adopted the the Philadelphia Confession in 1767, but it was not the first, nor the only one, to do so in America. Its "Summary of Church Discipline", published in 1774, reflected the influence of the view of eldership held by Benjamin Keach and John Gill, which, as we have stated already, was responsible in its measure for the decline to the one-pastor-many-deacons situation in later Baptist life. Chanski and his colleagues will need to shout "plurality" louder in order to prevent their view of the eldership from sliding down the same slippery path!

3.1.3 Poh and Owen

Chanski proceeds to compare my view of the eldership with that of John Owen's. He claims that

"Poh follows Owen to a point (p. 101)", while Sam Waldron claims that "Poh follows Owen to a fault (p. 53)." Chanski insists that I believe "that elders who labour in the word have a higher degree of authority than elders who do not labour in the word (p. 108)", that I believe that "the one who labours in word and doctrine has greater *governing authority* (p. 109)", that I believe that the teaching elder "has *de jure* authority above that of the non-teaching elder(s) (p. 112)". I believe no such thing.

Chanski's propensity at misrepresentation shows again when he claims that I had difficulty finding explicit support from John Owen for the view that the teaching elders have "greater *governing authority*" over the ruling elders (emphasis his, p. 109). He says, "Poh evidently senses this when he attempts to enlist support for his assertion from Owen. He appears to realise that he has no explicit support from Owen here and that the strongest statement he can make is that there are *some indications* that Owen did believe in 'the priority of the ministry' in the sense in which he (Poh) understands it." What I was establishing was "the priority of the minister", which is different from "the greater governing authority of the minister". I mentioned that Owen did not explicitly teach the principle of the priority of the ministry because there was no reason for him to do so, since this principle was already in recognition and it needed no defence (p. 122 of my book). I then proceeded to show that there are indications, nevertheless, that Owen believed in the priority of the ministry. I said, "Below are some indications that Owen did believe in the priority of the ministry" (p. 123 of my book). A total of fourteen passages from John Owen, grouped under five sections, followed. The phrase "some indications" clearly means "some of the many indications", whereas Chanski makes it to mean "there are only some indications". Chanski! Chanski!

Chanski further claims that I differed from Owen on who is to preside in the elders' meetings (pp. 112-113). I ground the teaching elder's chairmanship in "the priority of the ministry", whereas Owen cited other factors in the determination of who is to preside. Chanski quotes Owen, to show that he allowed for the elders to "take turns" at this duty, and that he consistently maintained the parity of authority. However, the context of those words from Owen needs to be noted. Owen was about to launch into a detailed discussion of the office of the pastor (which, to him, meant the teaching elder). Before he did so, he deliberately digressed to prove that the office of bishop, presbyter, or elder is one and the same, as opposed to the view of prelacy (Works, Vol. 16, p. 44). It was in this context that he emphasised the parity of authority among the elders, although advocating the necessity of one of them acting as chairman when there are many elders. The following points may be noted, which Chanski chooses to obscure:

(i) Allowing for the elders to "take turns" is not the same as advocating that this should be the case in every situation. The norm is to be distinguished from the exception. Similarly, in my view of the priority of the ministry, the minister should be the leading elder, but that does not exclude exceptional situations in which a senior ruling elder may act as chairman for a time.

(ii) Owen's "plurality of elders" was one made up of elders divided distinctly into teaching and ruling ones, in which the two distinct functions of teaching and ruling are distributed among them in the way he clearly spelled out. Even in the present section of his book, in which he digressed to prove that the office of bishop, presbyter, or elder is one and the same, the two distinct functions of teaching and ruling are made clear. He said, "I shall never oppose this order, but rather desire to see it in practice, – namely that particular churches were of such an extent as necessarily to require many elders, both teaching and ruling, for their instruction and government,..." (Works, Vol. 16, p. 46).

(iii) Owen was countering the claim of prelacy that the minister or bishop is an officer higher in authority than the presbyters or elders. He was not discussing the relative roles of the teaching and ruling elders yet. Immediately after that digression, he began to discuss the role of the pastor, saying: "The first officer or elder of the church is the pastor. A pastor is the elder that feeds and rules the flock, 1 Pet. 5:2; that is, who is its teacher and its bishop..." (Works, Vol. 16, p. 47). Owen did not minimise the special role of the pastor. Later on, when discussing the teachers in the church, he emphasised that there is "no difference... as unto office or power" between bishops and presbyters, at the same time advocating the leadership of "one pastor or bishop in one church, assisted in rule and all holy administrations with many elders teaching or ruling only (*ibid.*, p. 105)".

In these points, obscured by Chanski, lie our quarrel with the "parity" view: the "parity" view fails to give due recognition to the scriptural distinction between the teaching function and the ruling function, and between the teaching elders and the ruling elders. It also fails to give due recognition to the special role of minister of the gospel. Chanski begins his discussion by acknowledging that John Owen believed there is only one office of elders, in which are two sorts of elders – the teaching elders and the ruling elders. He also admits to "the peculiar calling and work of some elders to labour in word and doctrine'", claiming that "This is a scriptural distinction (p. 106)". But as he proceeds, he blurs that distinction and minimises the special role of the minister, by insisting that these are a mere matter of "diversity of functions" between the elders. Chanski has the temerity to claim that he and his colleagues "agree with Owen in substance, but not in form (p. 106)", that they "hold to Owen's views on the eldership *essentially*, differing from him basically in terminology (p. 114)".

Chanski wants us to believe that the moon is the sun.

3.2 Chap. 7. "The Baptist Confession of 1689 and the Parity of the Eldership", by Sam Waldron

Waldron shows forth his irritation that I had claimed in my book that the 1689 Confession is "crystal clear" in its teaching on the eldership. He attempts to support his opinion that one cannot be dogmatically clear about the view of eldership taught in the 1689 Confession by the following steps:

(i) Asserting that the distinction between teaching and ruling elders "is not derived and cannot be derived from the text of the Confession itself (p. 120)". But this is true only if the prior assumption is made that the pastors and the elders are to be absolutely equated, as has been done by Waldron and his colleagues, which I have pointed out in my book (p. 127 [128]). If, on the other hand, the terms "pastor" and "minister" in the 1689 Confession are understood to mean the teaching elders, Waldron's case crumbles.

(ii) Casting doubt on my view, by repeating much of what I have said concerning the differences between the Savoy Platform and the 1689 Confession, and then throwing in the statement: "These patent alterations in the Savoy Platform are very significant. Poh Boon Sing's attempts to explain them in light of the differing historical situations in which the two Confessions were written do not carry weight since the Particular Baptists in 1689 and the Independents in 1658 faced very similar situations (p. 122)." Where, and in what ways, had Poh Boon Sing attempted to explain the alterations in the light of differing historical situations? I had, in fact, explained them in the light of similar historical situations.

(iii) Harnessing Benjamin Keach's view of the eldership to support the idea that the Particular Baptists altered the Savoy Platform because of disagreeing that there is a sharp distinction between the ruling elders and the preaching elders. Yet, severe reservations and qualifying disclaimers are made over Keach's view of the eldership (p. 125)! This is what Waldron says:

3. HISTORICAL CONSIDERATIONS

"It is, of course, not certain whether other Particular Baptists understood 26:10 (of the 1689 Confession) or the eldership in exactly the way Keach did. It is also very unlikely that Keach's view that all pastors should be supported can be maintained in the light of Scripture. It is possible that there are other weaknesses in Keach's view of the eldership. A reading of his little book gives the impression that he was weak on the Bible's teaching that normally the government of the local church rests in the hands of a plurality of elders in each local church. However all this may be, it is abundantly clear that Keach rejected anything like a distinction between pastors and elders in the church."

Waldron's case in unconvincing. He totally ignores the arguments that I employed in support of my view that the 1689 Confession actually assumes that there is a sharp distinction between the pastors, who are the teaching elders, and the ruling elders (pp. 120-131 [120-132] of my book). I supported that claim by a historical consideration of the document, based on the Savoy Platform, the 1644 Baptist Confession, the Separatist Confession of 1596, and John Owen. I also referred to the fact that the Particular Baptists altered certain terms found in the Savoy Platform, to reflect more accurately their view. It was also pointed out that the 1689 Confession teaches that it is the prerogative of the preacher to administer the ordinances of baptism and the Lord's Supper, since the proof texts used in the original Confessions were those referring to preachers of God's word.

Waldron has not engaged in a "refutation" of my case, nor provided cogent "proofs" for his case. Instead, his arguments are very much of the nature of assertions, protestations, and tentative suggestions.

Chap. 9. The Practice of the Parity of the Eldership, by Dave Chanski

In this closing chapter of the book, Chanski persists in claiming that I hold to the view that the teaching elders have "supremacy or priority of authority in the rule of the church (p. 134)". He lists four weaknesses inherent in that view. Since that is not my view, the points he raises are irrelevant to our debate. He is, in effect, shooting at the straw-man that he has erected. We only wish to point out another case of the dubious way by which Chanski handles the debate between us.

Chanski, and Waldron, have made much of Benjamin Keach's view of the eldership to their advantage. Chanski now uses Keach in an unfavourable way to discredit me, saying: "Remember that Benjamin Keach saw neither scriptural warrant nor practical necessity for any other than preaching elders in the church. Dr. Poh similarly fails to appreciate the importance of pursuing the scriptural ideal at this point when he writes: 'The principle of "plurality" is being bandied about as a new form of "shibboleth". In the face of these new problems, it would not be wise to stress "plurality". No, it might not even be *right* to do so.'" Chanski continues by quoting a passage from Cotton Mather, which referred to the Reforming Synod in 1679, lamenting the situation in which churches had only one teaching officer, to drive home the importance of having a plurality of elders. He further quotes Owen to the same effect. What Chanski does not point out are the following:

(i) He is misrepresenting my position by selective quotation. Immediately after those words which he quoted from my book, I had written: "It is preferable to advocate instead the validity of the office of ruling elders. This would be a wider principle that encompasses the concept of "plurality", for when ruling elders are appointed to help the pastor, would not there be a plurality of elders? The plurality advocated by the early Independents, like John Owen, was one in which both teaching and ruling elders share the rule: not one in which only teaching elders bear the rule" (p. 159 [160-161] of my book). Indeed,

I also advocated "the unity of the eldership" in place of "the equality of all elders", in another chapter of my book (p. 173 [174]), which Chanski does not appear to have read.

(ii) In the Reforming Synod of 1679, the New England ministers were lamenting the absence of ruling elders and teachers to help the pastors (or teaching elders). Owen was similarly concerned that there should be officers other than the pastor to rule the church together. Theirs was a plurality that included teaching elders and ruling elders. Indeed, all the authors, except for Benjamin Keach and possibly R. C. H. Lenski, quoted by Chanksi and his colleagues, held to the view that there is a distinction between the teaching and ruling elders – a point not made clear by them.

(iii) Historically, it was the "parity" view of eldership, exemplified in Keach, that played a major role in the demise of the office of ruling elders (see p. 178 [180] of my book). Chanski now wishes to distance himself from Keach when, in fact, his view and that of Keach's are basically the same. They both share the idea that there is only one office of elder absolutely, in which is no sharp distinction between the teaching elders and ruling elders. They both deny the validity of the office of ruling elders. They both hold to the view that all the elders are pastors or bishops. The same passage from Keach's book has been quoted favourably by Chanski (p. 105) and Waldron (pp. 124, 125) in the earlier parts of the book. It is now being used unfavourably.

Chanski and Waldron want to have the cake, and eat it too!

3.3   Conclusion

The book,"In Defence of Parity", has failed to present a proper "restatement" and "refutation" of my view of the eldership. Instead, the "restatement" has been replaced with a serious misrepresentation of my view, and the "refutation" has been replaced by invectives leveled at my person and my view.

In the "statement" (or "proposition") of their view, the contributors have clearly spelled out what they mean by "parity" and "diversity". We have shown that theirs is an inadequate description of the biblical eldership, for the following reasons: (i) it fails to give due recognition to the priority of the ministry; (ii) it fails to show the biblical distinction between the teaching elders and the ruling elders; (iii) it uses terms ("parity", and "equality/diversity") that are too general and vague, that are consequential and not essential, and, therefore, cannot be made prescriptive to the churches without problems ensuing; (iv) it can only consistently uphold a doctrine of "the call to the ministry" that is different from the traditional view, and which minimises the priority of the ministry.

In the "proof" of their position, the contributors have offered unconvincing exegesis of two key passages of Scripture, namely Ephesians 4:11 and 1 Timothy 5:17. Their proof of "parity" and "diversity" is such that I can agree with much of what they claim, for these pertain to things that we hold in common, and are of a general nature. In the areas where we differ, the contributors have largely ignored the arguments I have used in support of my case, and engaged in misrepresentation and ridicule of my view.

The view of eldership propounded by these contributors may rightly be called "the Absolute Equality View", with no negative connotation implied or intended. It denies the principles of the priority of the ministry and the validity of ruling elders. This view of the eldership was responsible in its measure for the descent of churches to the one-pastor-many-deacons situation in the past.

My view of the eldership, which I have called the Independent View, takes into consideration all the relevant biblical data in a way not found in other views. A self-consistent view of the eldership emerges from the principles that constitute the Independent View, namely, "rule by elders", "the priority of the ministry", "the validity of ruling elders", "the unity of the eldership", and "rule with consent". These principles cover the full intent of earlier advocates of the Independent View, such as John Owen, and avoid the pitfalls spelled out by them.

It remains now to commend my book, "The Keys of the Kingdom", to those who have not read it. Those who have read "In Defence of Parity" will then be able to judge for themselves the merits, or demerits, of the present series of articles.

My aim throughout has been to seek a better understanding of the biblical teaching on church government, and in particular the biblical teaching on the eldership. I have restrained myself in my comments on those who differ from me, mentioning only those things which I believe right, true and necessary. If, in the process, of debate, unworthy words and attitudes have been displayed, it is much regretted.

= The End =